A LIFE OF AN ORDINARY BOY

AARAV DIXIT T- K- S

Be United

Contents

Foreword

Be Safe

Preface

Be Free

Acknowledgements

Be Good

Prologue

Be Perfect

1

A Life Of An Ordinary Boy

A boy with a simple life no school, no homework, etc. This is a world with no work, free money or ?? money we can say this is a very brilliant excellent outstanding bla...... life from your perspective. We can say this is an interesting life yes/no. The majority will say yes and some will say no but if there is no difficulty so what can be done without it, it is required in everything like in your video games so you cannot play in easy, medium, and our favorite hard. So, the difficulty is necessary for everything Difficulty fills our life with thrill and fun. Laziness is not fun at all tell me you can do any work by sitting at a place for the whole life, of course, No!, no joy, no thrill, no suspense at all!. This is a Life Of An Ordinary Boy.

Nothing should be copied at all.By Aarav Dixit Or Aarav's Bag The Khaitan School

See You Soon! Thanks For Reading

So guys take care my new book will publish soon bye ?

www.ingramcontent.com/pod-product-compliance
Lightning Source LLC
Chambersburg PA
CBHW022048150726
47990CB00004B/1657